Orcas Around Me
My Alaskan Summer

To Taiga and Ryland. D.P.

To my mother, Leila R. Bowman. L.B.

Orcas Around Me
My Alaskan Summer

Debra Page

Illustrated by **Leslie W. Bowman**

Albert Whitman & Company ✦ Morton Grove, Illinois

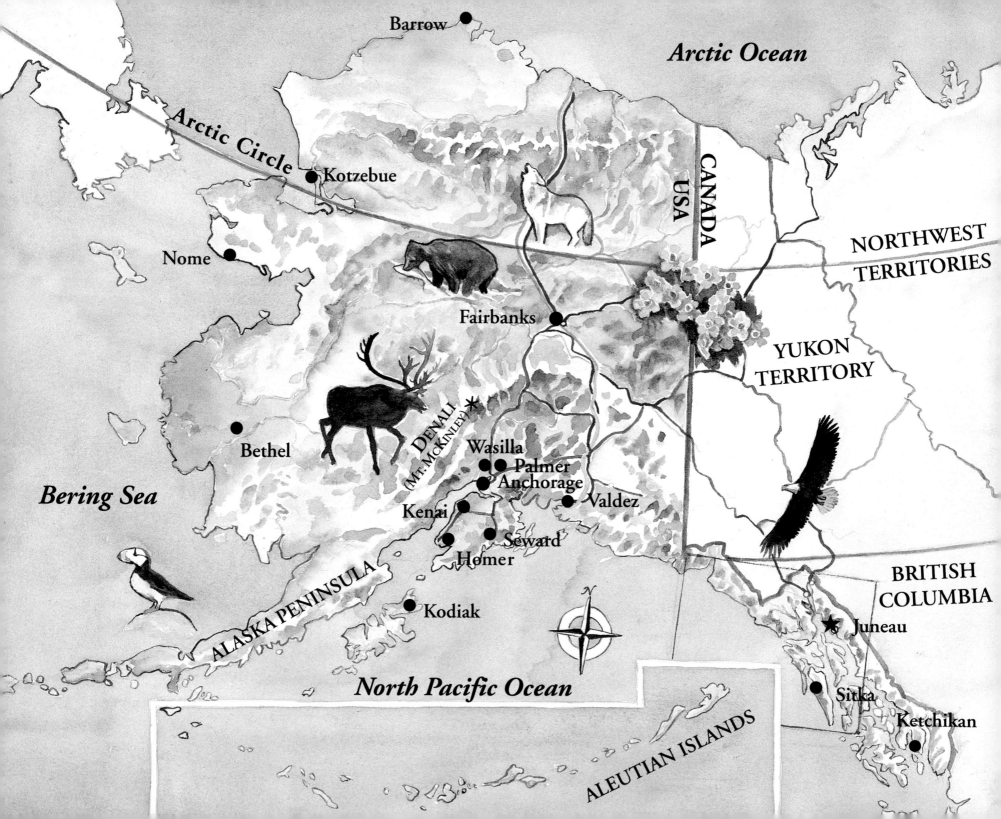

Arctic Ocean

Arctic Circle

Barrow

Kotzebue

Nome

Bethel

Bering Sea

ALASKA PENINSULA

Fairbanks

DENALI (MT. MCKINLEY)

Wasilla
Palmer
Anchorage

Kenai

Homer
Seward

Valdez

Kodiak

North Pacific Ocean

ALEUTIAN ISLANDS

CANADA
USA

NORTHWEST
TERRITORIES

YUKON
TERRITORY

BRITISH
COLUMBIA

Juneau

Sitka

Ketchikan

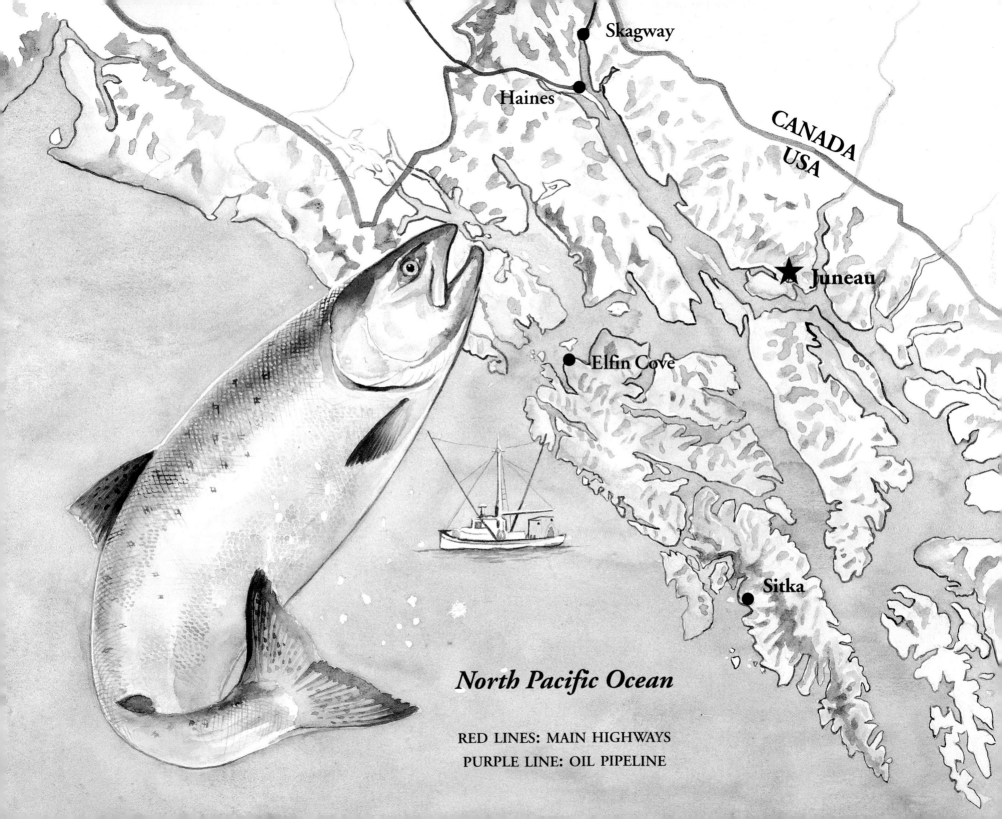

Skagway

Haines

CANADA
USA

★ Juneau

Elfin Cove

Sitka

North Pacific Ocean

RED LINES: MAIN HIGHWAYS

PURPLE LINE: OIL PIPELINE

My name is Taiga, the same as Alaska's northern forest. I was born in Alaska and for most of the year, I live and go to school there, in Fairbanks.

In the summer, I leave Fairbanks for the North Pacific Ocean of Southeast Alaska. My mom's and my dad's work is fishing for salmon.

I like to run on the sand beaches or hunt in the shallow pools for hermit crabs, blennies, and tiny codfish the size of my thumb. I also like to row my own skiff, the *Cat's Paw*. But I spend most of my time on a fishing boat with my brother, Ryland, and Mom or Dad.

We troll for salmon. That means we drive our boats around with a lot of hooks in the water and wait for the fish to bite. We wake up to the purr of the engine and when the fishing is good, to the slap of salmon coming aboard. At night, we drop anchor in a protected cove and make dinner, watch the sun set over the Fairweather Mountains, and look for the sea otters on their evening hunts.

Dad gave me the *Cat's Paw* last year for my seventh birthday. It took a while to learn to row it. First we had to find oars my size. Then I practiced with Dad. I could turn okay, but it was hard to go straight. I'm stronger now, so it's getting easier. Dad says Ryland and I can row anywhere as long as we wear life jackets and stay in sight of his boat. Sometimes I even let Ryland row. He's only three and so small I have to keep my hands on the oars with his or he dumps an oar overboard.

Ryland always fishes on Mom's boat, the *Man of Aran*. Since I'm older I can fish with my dad if I want. Dad's boat, the *Gunvor*, is bigger and more comfortable, but Mom tries to quit early each day so we kids can get time off the boat. Dad often fishes in rough weather or offshore where I don't want to go. If they both fish the same area, I take turns.

The *Man of Aran* is twenty-six feet long. Inside the cabin we share the bunk with our toys and extra clothes. Squiggly fishing lures hang on the cabin walls, and our damp clothes smell fishy hanging to dry above the stove. Outside, we play in a covered space next to the captain's chair. I color, play with clay, and read.

Sometimes, to be by myself, I climb on the cabin roof. From there, I can see forever. When it's sunny, Mom puts my brother up on top with me. She tethers him to the mast so he can't fall off. When the humpback whales or minkes or killer whales are feeding nearby, the roof is the place to be. "Whales!" was one of Ryland's first words.

One major boat rule: we always wear our life jackets unless we're in the boat cabin. Ryland doesn't like it, but I hardly notice anymore. I'm a good swimmer, but the water is so cold, about forty-five degrees Fahrenheit, and the currents so strong, it would be bad to fall in without a life jacket.

I did once, when I was Ryland's age. Mom was docking her boat in Elfin Cove to sell her fish. I'd taken my life jacket off when she wasn't looking. As she pulled up, I tried to jump from the boat to the dock. I missed. I don't remember, but Mom says she didn't know if I'd come up under her boat, under the dock, get crushed between them, or sink to the bottom. As she lunged over the side, she saw my head coming to the surface and grabbed me. She dunked me in a hot shower, and after that I always wore my life jacket.

Sometimes I help with the work. There's lots to do! I pump the bilge, where water settles in the bottom of the boat. I move fish into the storage tank and even pull fish into the boat if they're not too big or too wild. One time I landed a fifteen-pound king salmon.

A few days ago, Mom caught a herring as long as my hand. It was still alive so she put it into a tub of water. My brother laughed and pointed as we watched it swim. Then he tried to catch it in his hands and fell into the tub up to his shoulders! Mom had to take him to the cabin to change his clothes. Then we scooped the herring back into the ocean and saw it swim away. Ryland was mad at losing it. He didn't understand that it would die if we kept it. It's not fair to kill things we're not going to use.

That was the same day Mom got mad at the sea lion.

Sea lions eat salmon, too. In fact, a sea lion can eat a lot of salmon. And they know about fishing boats. One of them waited for us at Nibble Rock, the place salmon always bite. As we trolled past, he followed our boat. He swam underwater and snatched a big silver salmon right off our hook. Then he came up behind us, gulping and belching, with the salmon tail still sticking out of his mouth. It looked as if he was laughing at us.

Mom tried to pull in another fish before the sea lion got it. He beat her to that one, too. She was stomping mad, yelling, "I need a bottle rocket. That would scare you away, you thief!"

With no fireworks, she tried another trick. She drove her boat close to a big boat whose captain she didn't know. The sea lion knew there might be more fish on a bigger boat's lines and left us alone.

The *Gunvor,* Dad's boat, is thirty-four feet long. A bright orange buoy ball hangs from the boom as a swing for me. Sometimes it feels good to be on the *Gunvor,* free of my little brother.

Dad taught me to clean fish. We have to clean each fish as soon as we bring it on board. Our fish go to the best restaurants and markets all over the world so we take care to keep them fresh. We take out the gills and the insides, then scrape out the blood and rinse each fish with a hose. Once it's clean, we put it in a tub of seawater. This soaks out the last of the fish blood. When Dad has filled the tub with fish, my job is to move them into the storage hold. It's full of ice and saltwater so the fish will stay cold until we sell them. Some days my dad cleans hundreds of fish. He's very fast.

Mom worries about me using the sharp knives on the rocking boat. But I'm careful.

Sometimes dall porpoises come to play with our boat. They race us, diving under the bow. They zoom like black-and-white torpedoes. Dad says to lean over the bow and talk to them. They like the attention. Sometimes one turns on its side to look up at me with a bright black eye as it dives past.

Porpoises are mammals like whales and seals and us. They breathe air and have milk to nurse their babies. Some people say porpoises are almost as smart as humans. People study porpoise language, and try to teach porpoises to talk.

My dad tells a good porpoise story. It happened before I was born. While Dad was fishing with our old dog, Akimu, he hooked a porpoise by accident. The line went wild, swinging so hard he thought it would break. He pulled it up, surprised to see a porpoise with a hook in its mouth. He tried to talk to it, hoping it would know he was trying to help. That didn't work—the porpoise was thrashing so much Dad couldn't get his hand near the hook. Then Akimu leaned over the side of the boat and made a strange sound, almost like singing. Dad had never heard a dog make a sound like that before.

The porpoise stopped thrashing and lay still. Dad reached into its mouth and pulled out the hook. The porpoise swam away.

Mom likes to fish near a seal rookery on a rocky island. A rookery is the place where many seal families live together. At least a hundred seals lie on the rocks sunbathing all day long, unless they're off fishing. Since they're the same color as the rocks, they are well camouflaged. To see them, we tell Mom to drive her boat close; then I yell and whistle. We watch their rubbery bodies wriggle off the rocks and splash into the water. Dark round heads with big black eyes pop up around us.

Once we saw the killer whales hunt at the rookery. Three of them leaped high above the water after the seals. The seals climbed high on the rocks to get away. The whales' leaping made waves. The waves washed over one rock, and the seal that was lying on it disappeared. Later, there was blood in the water.

Killer whales, or orcas, are the most beautiful animals in the ocean. They're as big as Mom's boat and as fast as porpoises. The long fin on an orca's back juts out of the water like a black sword. They are very smart and they live in families, called pods, so they can work together when they hunt. My dad read a story from the newspaper about a killer whale that rammed a sailboat and sank it. Mom doesn't believe it. She says killer whales don't attack people, only seals and fish and other whales.

We had one wild adventure with orcas this summer. Mom and Dad decided to fish together in a new area. It was a long drive to get there, and Ryland and I fell asleep.

I woke when I heard a bump. The boat teetered to one side in slow motion. We had run aground on a rock. As a new wave rolled under us, it lifted the boat for just a second. Dad roared the engine. I heard a raspy sound underneath us, and we floated free.

My dad had taken a wrong turn. We'd come free of one rock, but we were lost in shallow water with no room to turn the boat around. It was one of those times when I knew I should stay out of the way.

"Drop the anchor," Dad told Mom. "We can put in the *Cat's Paw* and look for a way out." I heard the splash as Mom pushed the anchor overboard.

"Hey look!" she yelled. "Killer whales!"

I put on my boots and went up to see.

The big male's dorsal fin stood as tall as my dad. From just a few boat lengths away that bull orca watched us, while a female and a calf swam as fast as submarine missiles. The whites of their bellies flashed in the dark water. They came right at us.

They circled the boat.

I mean, *they touched our boat with their bodies!* They swam on top of the water, rolled against us, watched us with their black eyes. Going around the stern they bent their bodies to fit the curve of the boat so they could keep rolling against us. I could have reached out and patted one, if I could have moved. They rolled and touched and watched us. When the mother's head passed our stern, her tail reached the front cabin. She was two-thirds as long as our boat and almost half as wide!

"I've never been so close before," Mom whispered. I don't think she could move, either.

Then the two swam back to the big male.

Dad said, "Maybe that wasn't a rock we hit, but their baby."

"Maybe we're in their nest. Do orcas have nests?" Mom asked.

"Look!" I squeaked. "They're all coming back."

Dad grabbed the aluminum pole we use to catch things that fall overboard. He stood on the side of the boat and lifted the pole like a harpoon.

The orca bull came at us.

I looked at Dad. I looked at the whale. Mom looked at Dad and started to laugh. There he was with that bendy little pole ready to fight that huge killer whale. We waited.

About ten feet from the boat, the three whales veered and swam past us. They stopped on the other side of the boat to look once more. Then they swam away.

I breathed again.

Dad was afraid to put in the *Cat's Paw* to search for the passage out. He said the whales made him feel small. For me, it seemed like the human beings and whales had switched places. We have always been the ones to catch fish, but now, for a minute, it seemed like those killer whales might catch us. They could have if they'd wanted.

When the tide rose, we had enough water to reach the main channel. My little brother had slept through the whole thing.

Meeting the killer whales scared me. Not the kind of scared that could keep me away from the ocean, just the kind that makes me cautious.

Living here in Alaska, I am cautious even where the water is calm and safe. If Mom and Dad anchor the boats at Magic Beach during a slow tide, Ryland and I climb into the *Cat's Paw*. I check our life jackets and the breeze and the current. I catch Mom watching us through the boat window.

Then I know I can concentrate on finding our favorite sea otter. He lives in the kelp around Striped Rock. The weedy kelp is brown with round parts that look like otter heads and long streamer parts that look like otter flippers. He has good camouflage there.

He'll dive to the shallows and catch a crab or a clam. They're his favorite food. While he's down, he'll pick up a small rock, too. Then, floating on his back, he'll bang the rock on the shell he holds against his furry belly. Clap! Clap! The sound echoes from the rock cliffs. Ryland will jump to look around. When we find our otter, he looks like a little whiskered man sneaking close through the water. He's curious about us, too.

When he sees us, he stands on his tail with his strong back flippers until his chest and belly clear the water. He likes it when I whistle to him. If I row too close, he dives. He can swim underwater a long way and come up anywhere. Then we have to look for him all over again.

When we're done fishing, we drive our boats to Elfin Cove to sell our fish.
Elfin Cove is a village with twenty-four houses. There are no roads or cars, just
a boardwalk along the edge of the water. People can only get to Elfin Cove by
boat or floatplane. In summer, the store and the inn open for the fishermen. In
winter, the one-room schoolhouse has nine students.

The fish-buying scow is the busiest place in Elfin Cove. When we pull up,
Randy, the head of the fish-buying crew, grabs a line to tie us up. His helpers get
the equipment ready to take our fish. A mechanical hoist lowers into our boat to
lift the bags that hold our fish. Randy sorts the fish and weighs them, then pays
Mom or Dad. After we scrub the boat clean, the scow dumps ice in our hold for
tomorrow's fish.

Most of the fish we caught will travel on a bigger boat to Seattle. Some will
be sold in the United States; some will be flown to markets in France and Japan.

$\mathcal{M}$y favorite time is the end of the day. Once we drop the anchor, it's so quiet we can hear the slap of the water on the hull, a breeze in the rigging, an eagle screak. In Dad's boat cabin it's warm, and the dinner smells are delicious. Dad says, "Guess what we're having tonight."

I smile. I know the answer. "Fish."

Wildlife ✧ Glossary

---

blenny or **eelblenny** · The eelblenny is an eel-like fish that lives in cold waters off the Alaska coast. Along their backs are feathery fins that have tiny spikes. Finger-length blennies are often found in tide pools.

cod or **codfish** · A fish with five fins found in both the Atlantic and Pacific oceans. It is often used for food. Gray cod, a true cod, grow three feet long and weigh ten to twenty pounds. Ling cod look prehistoric with their large, toothy mouths and long, tapered, orangish bodies covered with dark speckles. Sablefish, or blackcod, can be found in water as deep as nine thousand feet. Cod fingerlings, or baby cod, live in the shallows along the Alaskan coast and are often found in tide pools.

crab · An animal with a very hard shell and ten jointed legs. Crabs live in or near water. A hermit crab is a small crab that uses its back legs to hold an empty snail shell, in which it lives. The Dungeness crab, tanner crab, and the Alaska king crab, which can weigh up to twelve pounds, are good to eat.

herring · A small fish that travels in huge schools, or groups. When herring come to the coast in the spring to lay their eggs, or spawn, people catch them for their roe, or eggs. Salmon love to eat herring.

orca or **killer whale** · A toothed whale that belongs to the dolphin family. Killer whales can be thirty feet long and weigh up to ten tons. They can swim as fast as twenty-five miles an hour. Orcas live in all of the world's oceans, making them the most wide-ranging animal on earth. In Southeast Alaska, fish-eating pods can have thirty or more whales. Mammal-eating orcas run in smaller groups, often of only two or three whales. They eat seals, walrus, even swimming moose or deer. There has never been a verified attack on a human.

porpoise · Another member of the dolphin family. Porpoises grow to be about six feet long. A dall porpoise has a black body with white sides. Porpoises swim together and often follow boats. They are thought to bring luck to people who fish.

salmon · A fish that is popular as food and for sport fishing. Five kinds of salmon live in Alaska: chinook, or king; coho, or silver; sockeye, or red; chum, or dog; and humpback, or pink. Taiga's family fishes for all five species. Pinks are about fifteen inches long and weigh only about two and a half pounds. Most king salmon are about three feet long. They weigh from twelve to about seventy-five pounds.

Salmon hatch from eggs laid in streams and lakes. Soon after, they swim downstream to the ocean. For some, like the Yukon River salmon, the river journey can be 2,000 miles (3,200 kilometers). In two to five years, a salmon returns to the stream where it was born, there to lay its eggs and die. Some scientists say salmon smell their way home.

Pollution, dams, and destruction of stream habitat have hurt salmon stocks in Washington, Oregon, California, Idaho, and parts of British Columbia, Canada. In Alaska, salmon stocks are the strongest in twenty years because of good management.

seal · A mammal that spends much time in the water. With their sleek bodies and flippers, seals swim fast. Their fur and blubber, or fat, help them stay warm even in very cold water. Harbor seals eat small fish and octopi. They are much smaller than sea lions. Rookeries, usually on islands or rocks, are where seals gather to mate and have babies.

sea lion · An enormous kind of seal that has ears on the outside of its body and long, flat front flippers. Sea lions can walk and stand on their flippers. Male sea lions grow to eleven feet long and weigh about 1,250 pounds. Females are smaller, weighing only about 600 pounds.

sea otter · A furry mammal that lives in the North Pacific Ocean. Adults grow to be five feet long and weigh about eighty-five pounds. A sea otter swims, eats, and sleeps on its back in the water. It eats many kinds of sea creatures and can open clams by pounding them against rocks. In the 1800s, fur traders killed sea otters for their luxurious pelts, then the most expensive fur in the world. By the 1950s, there were no sea otters left in Southeast Alaska. Starting in 1965, the Alaska Fish and Game Department and the U.S. Wildlife Service imported 412 sea otters from the north to repopulate Southeast Alaska. Now, Alaskan sea otters thrive.

whale · A very large mammal that lives in the sea and looks like a fish. Like other mammals, whales are warm-blooded and give birth to live young. *Baleen* whales have no teeth. They feed mainly on tiny plants and animals called plankton. These are filtered through thin plates, called baleen, in the whale's mouth. Minke whales and humpback whales are baleen whales.

Toothed whales have teeth which they use to grab fish and animals. Orcas are toothed whales.

Whales have poor eyesight, but they can hear many sounds humans cannot. They communicate with underwater sounds, bouncing the sound off objects to find their location. This is called echo location.

A humpback whale can dive under water and hold its breath for forty minutes. When it surfaces, it exhales and breathes new air through a blowhole, which is a nostril on top of its head.

Debra Page

In 1977, I bought an outboard engine and a skiff. That was my first summer as an Alaskan fishing captain. Since then, I've gotten a larger boat that holds many more fish. I've learned more about the ocean. But I still travel the same areas of wilderness catching salmon. Both my sons, Taiga and Ryland, have grown up fishing with me or my husband. All the stories in this book are true.

When the salmon season closes, we return to Fairbanks for the school year. In the coolest months, my family travels. We've found the desert in Namibia, the mountains in Nepal, and the jungle in Sumatra as wild as our home in Alaska.

Leslie W. Bowman

So that I could illustrate *Orcas Around Me: My Alaskan Summer,* I traveled to Southeast Alaska. It's the most beautiful place I've ever seen. Debra Page and her family were generous enough to take me with them on their fishing boats and show me how they work and live. They also showed me whales, otters, and all the other wonderful life they see daily. I never thought I'd be in a place so wild.

I started to illustrate books in 1986, and since then I have illustrated seventeen books for children, including *The Fiddler of the Northern Lights* by Natalie Kinsey-Warnock. I live in Minneapolis, Minnesota, with my dog, Jazz.

Library of Congress Cataloging-in-Publication Data

Page, Debra.
  Orcas around me: my Alaskan summer / written by Debra Page; illustrated by Leslie W. Bowman.
  p. cm.
  Summary: A young boy describes his summers spent fishing for salmon with his parents and younger brother off the southeastern coast of Alaska.
  ISBN 0-8075-6137-1
  1. Salmon fishing—Alaska—Juvenile literature. 2. Killer whale—Alaska—Juvenile literature.
[1. Salmon fishing. 2. Family life—Alaska.] I. Bowman, Leslie W., ill. II. Title.
SH684.P34 1997
639.2'755—dc20   95-52647
                                                                        CIP
                                                                         AC

Text copyright © 1997 by Debra Page.
Illustrations © 1997 by Leslie W. Bowman.
Published in 1997 by Albert Whitman & Company,
6340 Oakton Street, Morton Grove, Illinois 60053-2723.
Published simultaneously in Canada by General Publishing, Limited, Toronto.
10 9 8 7 6 5 4 3 2 1
🐋 🐋 🐋
The display faces are Stone Serif
  and Kunstler Script Medium.
The text typeface is Garamond.
The illustrations are watercolor.
The design is by Karen A. Yops.